The Adventures of Kitty Cat

The Billion $$ Power Ball Winner

Vol 2

Women's March on Chicago 1/21/ 2017

Renee Blanche

The Adventures of Kitty Cat

The Billion $$ Power Ball Winner

Vol 2

Women's March on Chicago 1/21/17

First Edition, January 2017

Copyright (c) 2017 by Renee Blanche

Contact:
ReneeBlanche@aol.com

Printed by CreateSpace,
An Amazon.com Company
Available on Kindle and other book stores

ISBN-13: 978-1542751087
ISBN-10: 154275108X

Dedication

To my mother, Blanche,
who, at 95, voted for a woman president
for the first time

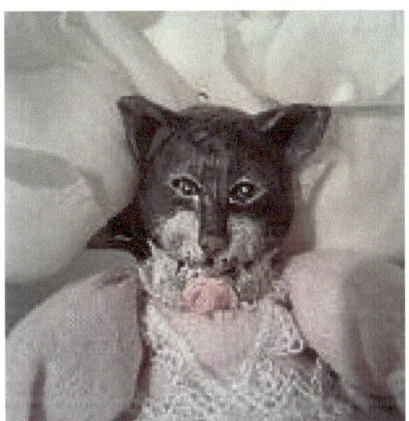

Acknowledgements

With thanks to Rachel and Vivienne, Linda, Jamie, Civia,
Brigid, Carol, and all the Women Marchers I met

January 21, 2017 in Chicago

EPISODE I

Kitty Cat was a pussy cat, but she had never been man-handled. She could run faster, scream louder, and/or dig her claws in deeper when someone threatened her. She was happy that she had recently won a billion dollars, but she was unhappy that a fellow billionaire had boasted that he could assault women: ". . . Grab them by the pussy. You can do anything."

"Hmmm," Kitty thought, maybe that is true. Her fellow billionaire could do what he liked. "Hmmm," she thought again. "I can, too." She knew that she might suffer consequences in doing what she liked, but if it's important enough, maybe suffering a consequence was not worse than giving up her rights as a pussy.

And that is why Kitty Cat went on the Women's March in Chicago on January 21, 2017.

She called Jamie, who had called Shelley. Both had won Emmys that year. Kitty thought, she'll see the Women's March through producers' eyes. Kitty could learn from them. Jamie said, "We will have to figure out where to meet and at what time. It's almost impossible to find someone in a large crowd." Reports online said about 25,000 people were expected to march.

Ahhh, logistics. How would Kitty get to the starting spot? She got out the map of the March, which was posted online. Hmmm, the March would start in Grant Park in Chicago, between Lake Shore Drive and Michigan Avenue. Kitty then thought: Is there anyone else I know who lives nearby? Then I would travel with her to Grant Park.

She called Linda, her photographer friend. Hmmm, Linda hated crowds, especially ones that could be filled with lots of trouble. Trouble. Kitty considered the problem. Once again she concluded that a little bit of courage combined with another's little bit of courage doubled the power of their courage. Who else? Kitty thought.

Rachel, dear Rachel, her friend from downstairs might want to go. Then they could ride together and maybe meet Jamie and Shelly. Rachel was the mom of a sweet 6 year old girl who had the beginnings of a fierce and funny woman.

 "Will you bring Vivienne?" Kitty asked Rachel.

"Maybe not," Rachel said. Kitty thought about whether she had the right to say what she was thinking, and then said to her friend, "It's probably the decision that a woman makes for herself when she is ready." Marching, ahhh, deciding to march, is each person's choice, each person's right.

 It was a sunny winter Saturday, and Kitty met Rachel in their building lobby. Her daughter, Vivienne, was there to see them off.

"I wish I could go," said Vivienne.

Rachel said, "You will march on another day."

Kitty looked at dear, sweet strong Vivienne. "I hope you won't have to," Kitty said.

Kitty had arranged a ride with her chauffeur to drop them at Lake Shore Drive and Jackson Blvd, one block from the Chicago bandshell on Columbus Avenue. There was no traffic and they were near the starting point in about 10 minutes. They saw people when they started walking west, but they were people dressed in uniforms: policemen, policewomen, some military garb that Kitty had never seen. Kitty tried to make eye contact with them, but they all looked away. Then Kitty saw the guns. All of them were carrying guns.

Guns. Hmmm

Guns and porta potties, lots of porta potties, stretched out along the Grant Park field.

And then they were there. They were there and a few others were there, maybe 500, maybe 1000, but it was already 8:45 am, and the speakers were scheduled to speak at the bandshell at 10 am. Would anyone else come to the Women's March of Chicago?

Rachel said as they stood on the outskirts, "I guess we're here." Kitty saw what looked like a speaker's bandshell, so she started walking towards it: "Let's get as close as we can." They walked to the fence where a woman was talking to her grown daughter who wore a pink pussy knitted hat. It was the type of hat Kitty had heard that so many were knitting all around the United States.

"Grab them by the pussy," Kitty remembered the words of the anti-feminist. A man can love his daughter, his mother, his wife, his wives, but if he does not respect them, he is only loving his reflection in their eyes.

And then Kitty called her friend, Jamie, who was meeting Shelly five blocks away. "We're stage left of the bandshell waiting for the speakers. We're on Columbus and Jackson," said Kitty. "There's no way I can make it to where you are," said Jamie. "But that's good news, because the streets are filled with marchers and more keep coming."

And then Kitty overheard the conversation behind her:

"It was 1968. My girlfriend, Eloise, was 24 years old, and she worked in a beauty parlor washing hair. 'I'm pregnant,' Eloise said one night. She was holding a coat hanger."

"A coat hanger?" Kitty heard.

"Yes, a coat hanger. Eloise was going to do an abortion herself."

"What happened?" the other marcher asked.

"I emptied my savings account of $300, drove her to a dark motel, and never forgot her crazed look as she returned to the car."

"No woman should have that experience."

"No woman should have that experience," said the woman who could not and would not forget. "And that is why we will never take a step backwards."

And that is when Kitty knew that what she was thinking, what she was feeling, was being felt by feminists, women who stood up for other women, women who marched for all women, women who marched for the rights of human beings and cats and all creatures to muddle through their lives, maybe with terror, maybe with courage, but deserving respect and inalienable rights to life, liberty, and the pursuit of happiness.

The best speaker in the bandshell was Sara Paretsky, a published author, who spoke of the work ahead. She was just one of a long line of speakers that included Aldermen, Congressmen, and representatives from Planned Parenthood and the ACLU, who said that this was just the beginning. (Kitty was surprised at herself that she felt comforted that the ACLU was in this fight, even though Kitty remembered that she had not always agreed with them.)

Then the announcement came around 11:10 am: "We cannot march--there are too many people-- we are a rally now of 150,000 marchers!"

Kitty wanted to move, but Rachel wanted to wait until 12:30 pm. In truth Kitty was getting a little bored, so she was happy when they slipped away from the massive crowd, but as they walked towards the Bean in Millennium Park and saw the marchers, Kitty's excitement grew. These others who could not fit on the space in front of the bandshell, well, they just decided to march anyway.

Kitty heard the beat of their rallying call: *Show me what democracy looks like . . . This is what democracy looks like . . . Show me what democracy looks like . . .*

Activists, organizers-- they knew what to do--and their calls were answered. This was Democracy. Kitty had lots of money, she was a billionaire, but Kitty knew that real power lay in her own conscience.

She committed in that moment to do the right thing even on a wrong day, an inconvenient day. That meant she would have to listen more to understand what the right thing was for her to do. Sometimes she would fail, she would make mistakes, but she pledged to make choices that helped others.

She heard the call:

"*Ain't no power but the power of the people, cause the power of the people don't stop . . .*" Kitty wasn't happy to use incorrect grammar, but she joined in anyway.

And she looked at the signs and was inspired by those who carried the weight with them throughout the march: *Pussy grabs back . . . Nasty women Don't Quit . . . My body My business . . . Pussy Power . . . Climate change is real . . . I will protect my rights . . . The Power of the People is Stronger than the People in Power.*

Standing next to Kitty in the crowd had been a young woman dressed like the Carrie Fisher Star Wars' character, Princess Leia.

Suddenly, Kitty heard her cry out: "That's me!" Another woman had made her resistance poster, a sign that people all over the world, people who had never met before, were all thinking very much the same thing about the world we can control. Maybe Kitty would think about making a sign the next time she marched.

EPISODE III

Jamie called when Kitty was in their cab taking them back to Lincoln Park. "Do you want to meet for dinner?" Jamie asked. "I have so much to share."

"Absolutely," Kitty said.

And that is how the two of them, Kitty and Jamie, began to draft their plan for being activists for the Women's Movement of 2017. Over plates of mussels and grilled calamari at Orso's in Old Town.

Rachel was part of it. And all her friends. And all of Kitty's friends.

And all of Jamie's friends. And all of their friends. And so it began. Jamie found Action Checklists on the internet, and Kitty said she would contact Amazon and Kindle. (And Kitty sent a check to the National Organization for Women.)

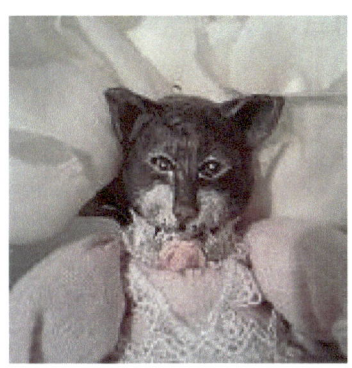

THE END

ReneeBlanche@aol.com

TIPS TO MARCHING

1. PACK ONLY YOUR ESSENTIAL NEEDS
2. PACK A SNACK
3. CHARGE YOUR PHONE AT HOME
4. WEAR LAYERS
5. WEAR COMFORTABLE WALKING SHOES
6. CHECK ONLINE REGULARLY FOR EXACT LOCATIONS, TRANSPORTATION, AND TIME CHANGES.
7. TRAVEL WITH A FRIEND FROM HOME
8. ONCE THE CROWDS FORM, YOU NEED A BACKUP PLAN WHEN YOU CANNOT FIND YOUR OTHER FRIENDS (Phone service may not work in a large crowd.)
9. BE COURAGEOUS
10. BE A PEACE MARCHER

ACTIVIST'S GUIDE

1. Find websites that speak to you.
(Be aware that you may not agree with all
of their positions.) You will learn, however,
details about your specific cause and how to
fight for that cause. (See ACLU, CREDO
Action and Elizabeth Warren's online
petitions below as examples of websites,
groups, and individuals advocating for
women's rights.)

2. C-SPAN is a 24 hour/daily primary
source for most of the news channels. It
may make you sleepy at first, but you will
hear exactly what your Senators and
Representatives say and not a newscaster's
shortened, opinionated version. They also
feature call-in shows asking for your opinion
(and opponents' opinions). And there are no
commercial breaks on C-Span.

3. Listen to the other side, and find ways
to communicate with those who do not
agree with you.

ENSURE THAT ILLINOIS ALLOWS FULL ACCESS TO REPRODUCTIVE HEALTH CARE

SUPPORT HB 40
Sponsors: Feigenholtz

For more information contact:
Khadine Bennett: 312.607.3355
kbennett@aclu-il.org
or Brigid Leahy: 217.
553.8976 brigidl@ppil.org

House Bill 40 strikes a dangerous "trigger" provision in the Illinois abortion law and affirms that Illinois will not go back to the pre-Roe days of illegal abortion.
.

By removing the anti-choice "trigger" language from the 1975 Act, HB 40 ensures that women's health care
will be protected in Illinois, regardl
ess of what happens to the Supreme
Court in a Trump administration.
There is simply too much risk.
HB 40 removes discriminatory provisi
ons from Illinois law that deny insu
rance coverage of abortion to
many women who depend on Medicaid and State Employee Health Insurance.
Every woman, regardless of whether she has private or
government-funded health insurance, should have
affordable and comprehensive health care coverage that
includes coverage for abort
ion care, so she can make
personal health decisions based on what
is best for her and her family.

State Employee Health Insurance
.

Aside from a narrow life exception, Illinois law bans abo
rtion coverage from non-contributory (employers
cover 100 percent of the premium paym
ents) state employee health plans.
.

Under current policy, state employees and their depend
ents are often denied coverage for reproductive
health care that is commonly available to those who
get their insurance in the private sector, including
denials of coverage for medically necessary abortions or
those required because of lethal fetal anomalies

Medicaid
.

Medicaid has restricted the use of
federal funds for abortion coverage to

cases of life endangerment, rape
or incest under what is known as the "Henry Hyde Am
endment." Under this policy,
health care providers are
often deterred from taking Medicaid as a form of
payment, because of the confusing web of exceptions
and restrictions that apply.

The "Henry Hyde Amendment" is not good policy.
Health programs for women with low incomes should
cover birth control, childbirth AND abortion care. All
women, regardless of income should have the same
right to decide if and when to have children.

Illinois should join the 15 states

that use state funds to provide wome
n with health assistance funds that
cover the full range of pregnancy-related care, includin
g a woman's decision to en
d a pregnancy. In this
time of budget crisis, it is important to note that
this bill would have zero cost for the Department of
Healthcare and Family Services (DHFS).
HB 40 respects that individuals and their fam
ilies need to make their own life decisions
When it comes to the most important decisions in life, like
whether to become a parent, it is vital that a woman is
able to consider all the options available to her. It is no
t our place to interfere with her decision by withholding
coverage. HB 40 is common sense policy that suppo
rts a woman's personal health care decisions.

These 15 states have policies t
hat allow state Medicaid funds to cover abortion
services: AK, CA, CT, HI, MD, MA, MN, MI, NJ,
NM,
NY, OR, VT, WA, WV.

ENSURE THAT ILLINOIS ALLOWS FULL ACCESS TO REPRODUCTIVE HEALTH CARE
SUPPORT HB 40

Sponsors: Feigenholtz
For more information contact:
Khadine Bennett: 312.607.3355
kbennett@aclu-il.org
or Brigid Leahy: 217.
553.8976 brigidl@ppil.

ENSURE THAT ILLINOIS ALLOWS FULL ACCESS TO REPRODUCTIVE HEALTH CARE
SUPPORT HB 40

Sponsors: Feigenholtz
For more information contact:
Khadine Bennett: 312.607.3355
kbennett@aclu-il.org
or Brigid Leahy: 217.
553.8976 brigidl@ppil.org

SUPPORTING ORGANIZATIONS
ACLU of Illinois
American Association
of University Women
Chicago Foundation for Women
Equality Illinois
EverThrive Illinois
Illinois Caucus for Adolescent Health
Illinois NOW
McHenry County Citizens for Choice
Mujeres Latinas en Accion
National Council of Jewish Women Illinois State
Policy Advocacy Network
Personal PAC
Planned Parenthood of Illinois

About CREDO Action

CREDO Action organizes for progressive change. We mobilize our 5 million activists to speak out and pressure decision-makers from the local to the national level. From opposing war, to relentlessly defending reproductive freedom, protecting our environment and a healthy food system, fixing our broken democracy, fighting for an economy that works for everyone, and more, CREDO empowers activists to work for the change we want to see, not what we are told we can achieve by Washington insiders.

CREDO Action is the activism arm of CREDO, a social change organization that offers products — like CREDO Mobile — in order to fund grassroots activism and progressive nonprofit organizations.

Over the course of our history, CREDO has donated over $82 million to Democracy Now!, Brennan Center for Justice, Doctors Without Borders, ACLU, EFF, Planned Parenthood, 350.org and hundreds of other nonprofit groups.

Our customers and activists have generated over 16 million letters and phone calls to elected officials, decision-makers and corporate headquarters across the country. Our activists have submitted their signatures over 137 million times on CREDO petitions and in public comments to government agencies.

We believe in the power of people coming together to make real change — no matter the odds. When we do, we can win.

Our activists have helped win historic victories for peace with Iran, real Net Neutrality, blocking the Keystone XL pipeline, Arctic offshore drilling and coal leasing on federal lands, raising the minimum wage, and blocking Wall Street cronies from political appointments — and that's just in the last couple of years.

from Credo

Stand with Sen. Warren: Make Trump disclose and divest

"Meaningless." That's how the director of the Office of Government Ethics described Donald Trump's recently announced plan to hold on to his business and ownership in hundreds of businesses with billions in assets and more than $600 million in debt.[1] It is now more important than ever to get behind Sen. Elizabeth Warren and the group of senate Democrats who have introduced a powerful new presidential conflicts of interest bill.[2]

With Trump's deep business ties to foreign governments and businesses, he will be in violation of the Constitution's rules against bribery on his first day in office. But federal conflict-of-interest rules contain a glaring loophole exempting the president and vice president from many restrictions. Sen. Warren's new bill would make it clear that Trump has to follow the rules – or else.[3]

A president using his power to enrich himself while indebted to foreign governments is not normal, and we cannot let Washington Democrats and the corporate media pretend it is. We need to get behind leaders like Sen. Warren and make it clear that Donald Trump is putting America's safety and security at risk in order to line his own pockets.

The federal watchdog's remarks on Trump's plan have Republicans talking about investigating or defunding his office.[4] It isn't the first time. The very first act of the new Republican Congress was an attempt to gut a similar independent office covering Congress, the Office of Congressional Ethics. But under massive public pressure, Republicans changed course within 24 hours. The whole episode was evidence that Trump Republicans are desperate to make corruption easier – and extremely vulnerable to public outrage on this exact issue.

Every modern president has voluntarily chosen to follow conflict-of-interest rules – until now. Even though those rules exempt the president and vice president, past leaders of both parties have divested their financial interests or placed them in a blind trust.[5] Trump merely intends to turn over day-to-day operations to his two sons while maintaining a financial stake in his business, which a bipartisan group of ethicists and good government groups has condemned.[6]

Trump's refusal to disclose and divest shows that he is intent on enriching himself and his Wall Street friends at the expense of Americans who struggle to make ends meet. This is the type of cronyism and corruption that conflict-of-interest rules are designed to prevent. Worse, his deep business ties to global financiers and the likes of China, Russia, Libya and Turkey put us all at risk. Trump has every incentive to make foreign policy decisions that benefit himself while putting American lives at risk.

Sen. Warren's new bill tackles Trump's potential corruption on both fronts. It would close the loophole allowing the president, vice president and their families to avoid conflict-of-interest rules – forcing Trump to disclose and fully divest his financial interests. It also emphasizes that the anti-bribery "emoluments clause" of the Constitution applies directly to situations like this, where the president's wealth is dependent upon pleasing foreign dictators.[7] This bill makes it absolutely clear that Trump's business ties put America at risk, so we need to get behind it in a big way.

Stand with Sen. Warren: Make Trump disclose and divest.

Thank you for speaking out.

http://chicagonow.org/new-stuff

Chicago NOW has five key issue teams that are dedicated to making our city a better place for women and girls. If you are interested in getting involved with the CNOW Action Team, email us at **chicagonow.org@gmail.com**. Our core issues are:

- [Reproductive Rights](#)

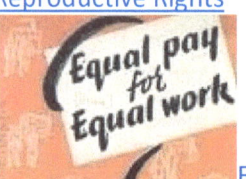

- [Economic Equity](#)

- [Stop Violence Against Women](#)

- [LGBTQ Rights](#)

- [Women's Health](#)